Pop-up London

A pop-up book to make yourself

Anne Wild

Contents:

1. The Tower of London and Tower Bridge

2. St. Paul's Cathedral and the Lord Mayor's Show

3. Trafalgar Square and Nelson's Column

4. The Houses of Parliament and Westminster Abbey

5. Buckingham Palace and the Victoria Monument

6. Central London, a visitor's guide

TARQUIN PUBLICATIONS

©1997: Anne Wild
©1983: First Edition
I.S.B.N.: 0 906212 30 8
Design: Wilson Smith
Printing: Ancient House Press, Ipswich

CE

Tarquin Publications
Stradbroke
Diss
Norfolk IP21 5JP
England

London is…

London is one of the most interesting cities in the world to visit. It is a city of pageantry and ceremony, where traditions going back hundreds of years are mingled with the life of a modern capital, where you will find royal palaces and famous sights, museums showing treasures from all over the world, art galleries and concert halls, churches and cathedrals, busy markets and quiet parks, a great river and sleepy canals, theatres, cinemas and hundreds of interesting corners, people and events.

Everywhere you will find traces of its long history. You can see the statues, memorials and graves of famous people and visit the places where important events happened. You can go to see the Crown Jewels or listen to speakers in Hyde Park. You can see 10 Downing Street, the Houses of Parliament or Buckingham Palace or take boat trips on the river or the canals. There are bus tours around the famous buildings and of course always the Underground or "Tube" to carry you from place to place.

Londinium, a settlement in Roman times, grew up around two low hills just north of the Thames. Today it is hard even to see them amongst all the buildings, but St. Paul's stands on the summit of one and The Bank of England on the other. Around these hills grew up the City of London itself, which even today occupies just one square mile. Nowadays the City of London is one of the major financial centres of the world and few people live there but in former times it was a warren of tiny, narrow streets teeming with people. That was until the Great Fire of London destroyed most of it in a few days. As the centuries have passed "The Great Wen," as Cobbett called it, has spread ever outwards until it has become one of the largest conurbations in the world.

In this book, the fascinating story of London is told in six pop-up scenes, a souvenir of a visit already made or perhaps an invitation card for the future.

HOW TO MAKE YOUR OWN POP-UP BOOK

You will see that some pages of this book are folded in an unusual way to give what are called 'wings', and on them are the pieces you need to make the pop-up scenes. On certain pages there are additional mini pop-ups as well as the main scene and you will find some extra pieces on a special page at the back.

TYPE OF GLUE

We particularly recommend a petroleum based glue like UHU or Bostick Clear. Good results can also be obtained with a white latex glue like Copydex. DO NOT USE a water based glue or paste which will cause the pages to buckle. If in doubt, do a small trial first.

SCORING

Paper is scored so that it will fold cleanly and pop-up crisply. The best method is to rule along the score lines with a ball-point pen which has run out of ink. Experienced model makers can use a craft knife, but it needs care not to cut right through the paper. Scoring is very important.

HOW TO PREPARE THE BASES

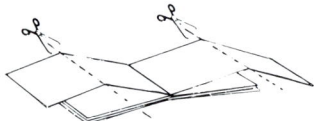

1. Open out the 'wings' and then cut them off along the folds. Cut off all 12 wings.
2. You will see at the back of the book a page of five minicovers. Remove it from the book by cutting along the printed 'cut' line.
3. You now have a book with a single blank page opposite these instructions, a single blank page opposite the instructions at the back and five pairs of facing blank pages. The next step is to glue each of the pairs of facing blank pages back to back to double the strength of the bases of the scenes. Do not cover up these instructions until you reach stage 6!

4. Spread glue smoothly about 1-1½ cm wide all round the edge on one of each pair. The blue tone on this page shows roughly the extent of glue needed. Gently press the pages together, starting at the spine and smooth outwards from the centre.
5. When all five pairs are done, the bases of scenes 2, 3, 4, 5, are ready and you can make up these scenes. See the instructions below.
6. When scenes 2, 3, 4, 5 are complete and these instructions are no longer needed, spread glue on the blue tone on this page and then glue it to the blank page opposite. Then you can make Scene 1.
7. When you have made up all the mini pop-ups and do not need those instructions any more, glue the blank back page similarly. Then complete Scene 6.

HOW TO ASSEMBLE EACH SCENE

The recommended order is to make Scene 4 first, then 5, 2, 3, 1 and finally Scene 6.

For each Scene.

1. Cut out each piece from the two wings keeping well away from the outline.
2. Score along all fold lines, dotted and solid.
3. Fold away from you to give a hill fold and towards you to give a valley fold. Crease firmly.

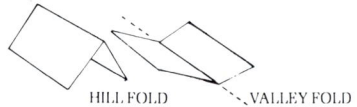

HILL FOLD   VALLEY FOLD

4. Cut out precisely.
5. For each scene there is a plan diagram which shows the position of the pieces. Start with piece 1 and work in order.
6. Each letter on a flap corresponds to a letter on the base or to a letter on another piece. Glue them in alphabetical order A, B, C, ...
7. Flaps marked 'glue behind', do not have a corresponding letter printed behind, but where there is any possibility of such a flap being glued in the wrong position, there are black lines on the base to help with alignment. This occurs in Scene 3.

POP-UP SCENE 1 THE TOWER AND TOWER BRIDGE

For a colour photograph of the completed scene, see inside the back cover.

Looking across the river Thames towards the north, this scene shows two famous London landmarks, the Tower and Tower Bridge. In the foreground two boats take some visitors down river while the bridge is opened for a larger ship to pass. Three mini pop-ups tell the stories of the execution of Anne Boleyn, the Beefeaters and Greenwich.

THE TOWER

Seen here looking north across the river, the Tower of London actually consists of twenty different towers joined by ramparts and fortifications. It is a formidable fortress and can lay claim to bèing one of the most historic buildings in England.

The Tower is guarded by Yeoman Warders who are usually called 'Beefeaters.' This sounds a very English name, but it really comes from the Norman French "Boufitier," or keeper of the King's Buffet. The ceremonial dress on the left was designed in Tudor times and is worn on special occasions. The pike he is carrying is known as a 'partisan.' The beefeater on the right is wearing the usual daily dress which was designed in Victorian times. He is holding one of the famous ravens which originally served as scavengers and are not at all friendly.

THE EXECUTION OF ANNE BOLEYN

This scene shows the execution of Anne Boleyn the second wife of Henry VIII and the mother of Queen Elizabeth I. The usual method of execution in those days was beheading, using an axe and block. In the Bloody Tower you can still see the original ones used at the Tower. However, Anne Boleyn requested that a sword be used instead and a special swordsman was brought over from France to carry out the execution.

It is said that to this day the Bloody Tower is haunted, because of all the dreadful deeds which were done there, and that the ghost of Anne Boleyn still walks "with her head tucked underneath her arm."

THE CEREMONY OF THE KEYS

Every night, just before ten o'clock there is a formal locking up of the Tower, known as "The Ceremony of the Keys." It is possible to obtain a pass to watch it, by written application in advance.

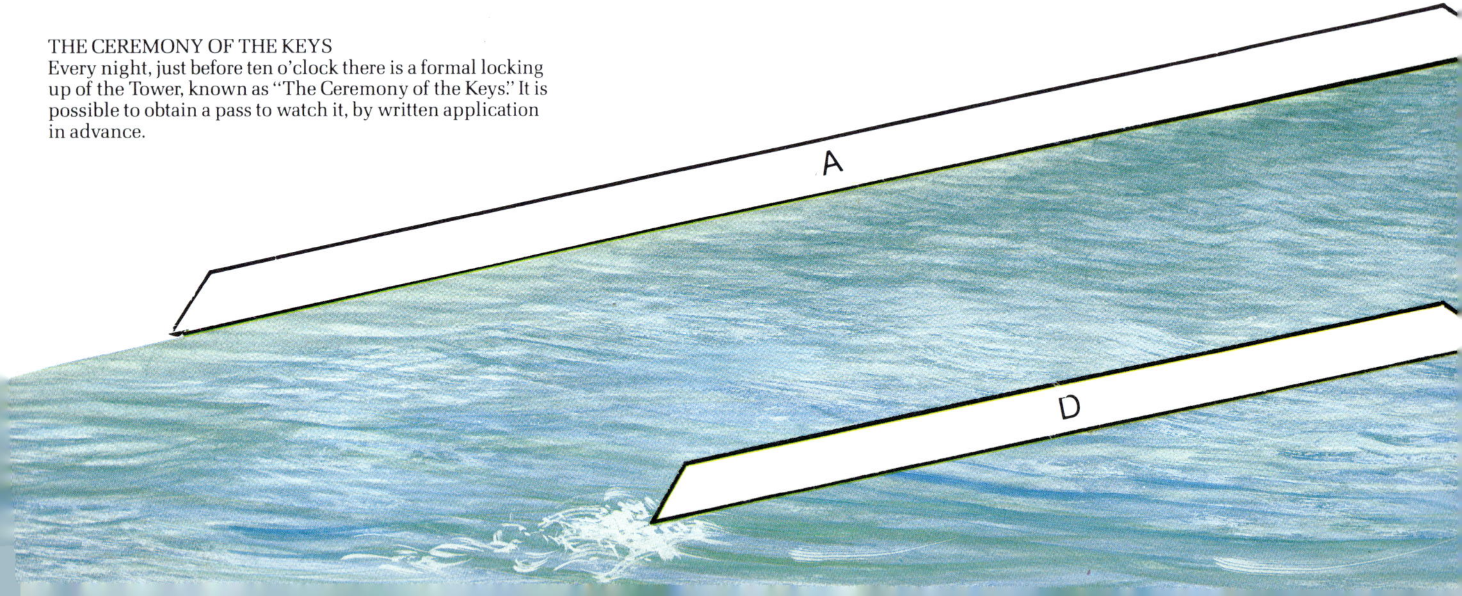

A

D

THE CROWN JEWELS

This marvellous collection of jewels is the royal regalia built up since the restoration of the monarchy in 1640. The earlier collections were mostly sold or melted down in the time of Cromwell and new ones had to be made for the coronation of Charles II.

They are kept in a deep vault under the Waterloo barracks at the Tower. Most visitors are not only impressed by the jewels themselves but also by the precautions taken to keep them safe. Only once has anyone succeeded in stealing the crown jewels from the Tower, a certain Colonel Blood in 1671. But he only got as far as the river bank before being arrested and the jewels were recovered. Charles II was so impressed by his bravery and audacity that he pardoned him, gave him a pension and allowed him to live at Court.

GREENWICH

One of the finest groups of buildings anywhere in England is to be found at Greenwich. They house the National Maritime Museum which tells the story of sea-faring through the ages with all kinds of exhibits and models. On the hill behind, stands the Old Royal Observatory which is the source of 'Greenwich Mean Time.' You can see the meridian line, a working planetarium and many kinds of telescope and other astronomical instruments.

Nearby, on the banks of the river are two historic vessels, the Cutty Sark and the Gipsy Moth IV, which are also open to visitors.

TOWER BRIDGE

This striking bridge, often used as a symbol of London was built in 1894. It is what is known as a Bascule Bridge because the roadway can be lifted up in two leaves to allow ships to pass. You can stand with one foot on each leaf and look down through the gap to the river below, but do choose a time when it is closed! The upper walkway is now open to the public and there are fine views of the river from it.

RIVER TRIPS

An interesting way to see a different aspect of London is to take a boat from Westminster Pier. There are daily services up river to Kew Gardens, Richmond and Hampton Court and down river to Tower Bridge and Greenwich.

You can also visit H.M.S. Belfast, an 11,500 ton cruiser, which is moored opposite the Tower of London.

THE TOWER OF LONDON AND TOWER BRIDGE

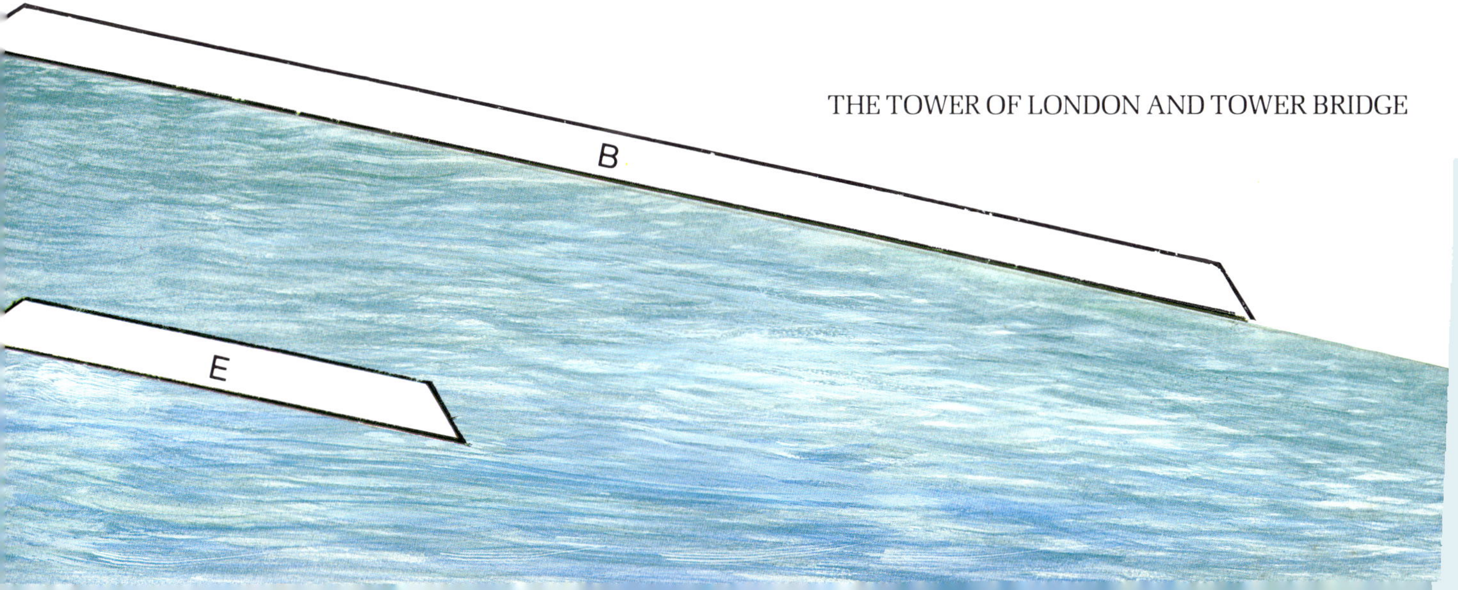

B

E

THE TOWER OF LONDON AND TOWER BRIDGE

SCORE VALLEY FOLD

F
GLUES BEHIND

SCENE 1
PIECE 3
D

SCORE HILL FOLD

SCENE 1
PIECE 6
J

SCORE HILL FOLD

G

SCORE HILL FOLD

SCENE 1
PIECE 4
E

SCORE HILL FOLD

SCORE HILL FOLD
H
SCORE HILL FOLD

SCENE 1
PIECE 7
I
GLUES BEHIND

SCORE HILL FOLD
L
SCORE HILL FOLD

SCENE 1
PIECE 10
M
GLUES BEHIND

SCORE VALLEY FOLD

C
GLUES BEHIND

N22

SCORE HILL FOLD

SCENE 1
PIECE 2
B

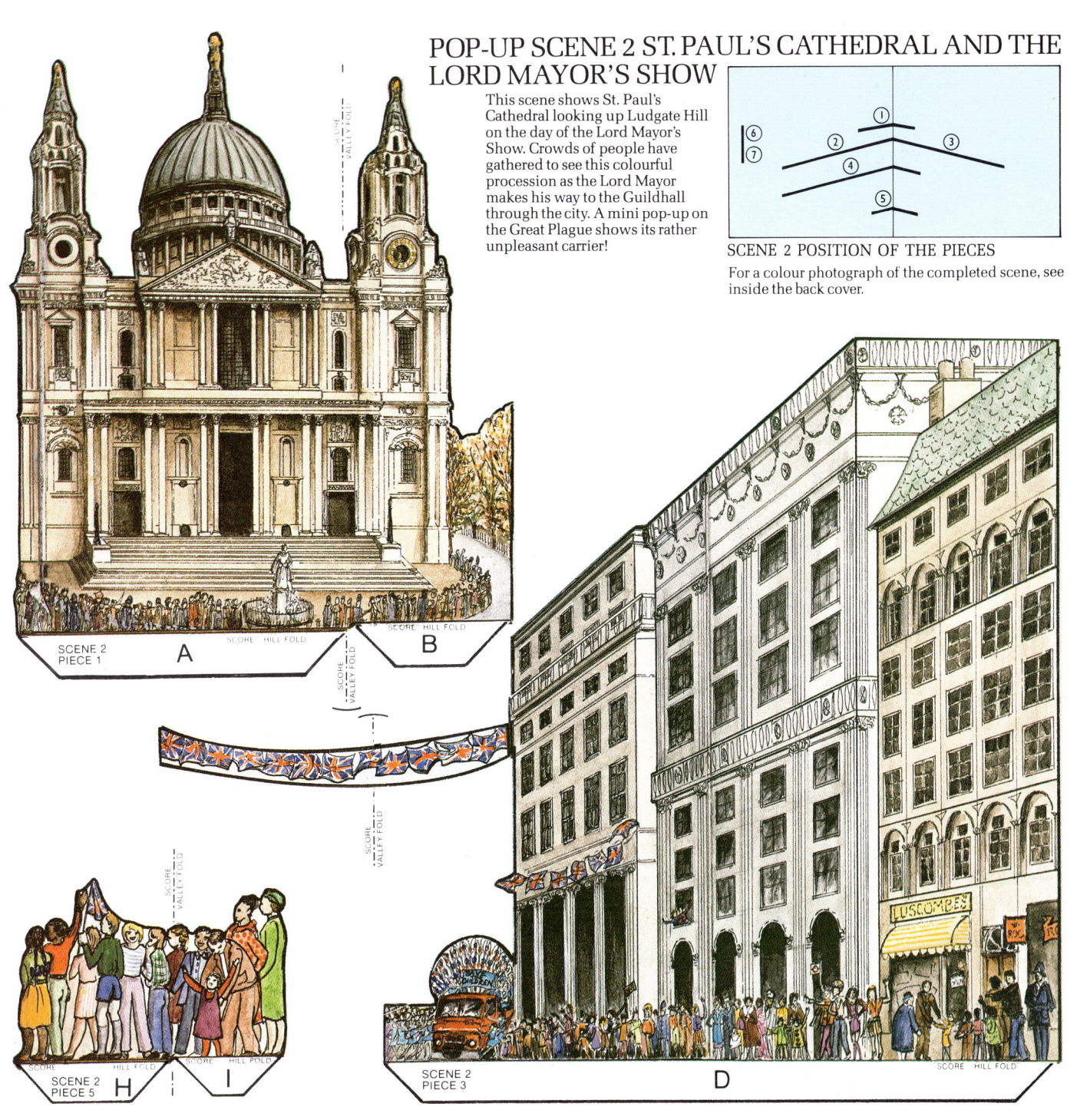

POP-UP SCENE 2 ST. PAUL'S CATHEDRAL AND THE LORD MAYOR'S SHOW

This scene shows St. Paul's Cathedral looking up Ludgate Hill on the day of the Lord Mayor's Show. Crowds of people have gathered to see this colourful procession as the Lord Mayor makes his way to the Guildhall through the city. A mini pop-up on the Great Plague shows its rather unpleasant carrier!

SCENE 2 POSITION OF THE PIECES

For a colour photograph of the completed scene, see inside the back cover.

SCENE 2 PIECE 1   A

B

SCORE HILL FOLD

SCORE HILL FOLD

SCORE VALLEY FOLD

SCORE VALLEY FOLD

VALLEY FOLD

SCORE VALLEY FOLD

SCENE 2 PIECE 5   H

I

SCORE   HILL FOLD   SCORE   HILL FOLD

SCENE 2 PIECE 3

D

LUSCOMBES

SCORE   HILL FOLD

ST. PAUL'S CATHEDRAL

This view of St. Paul's looking up Ludgate Hill, shows the west entrance of this magnificent cathedral on the day of the Lord Mayor's Show. It is the fifth cathedral dedicated to St. Paul on this site and was built by Sir Christopher Wren in 1675-1707 after "Old St. Paul's" was destroyed in the Great Fire.

It is not until you enter St. Paul's that you really appreciate the size of the dome and what a feat it was to build it. High up inside the dome is what is known as the 'Whispering Gallery.' Although it is 33 metres in diameter, it is easy to hear a whisper from the other side if you place your ear a few inches from the wall. Higher still is what is known as the 'Stone Gallery' and above that the 'Golden Gallery.' Both can be visited at certain times and there are fine views over the city.

In the crypt there are the graves or memorials of many famous people. Apart from Christopher Wren himself, Nelson and Wellington, more than 300 people are commemorated. It is fascinating to walk round and see the names of so many people who have played an important part in the history of their country. Also in the crypt is Wren's actual model of his second design for the Cathedral. He later said that is was the best work he ever did, bedore or since. However, like his first design, it was not accepted by the Commissioners because they said it was 'not traditional.' The third design, which was the one actually built, was based on it and it is interesting to compare the two. You can also see a model of 'Old St. Paul's' and a few other blackened relics which survived the Great Fire.

THE GREAT FIRE OF LONDON

In 1666, a fire in Pudding Lane, not far from London Bridge, spread out of control under the influence of a strong north-easterly wind and after four days, most of the old city was burned down. Although it seemed terrible at the time, in many ways it was a blessing in disguise because it swept away all the old insanitary streets and at last brought the Great Plague to an end. In the picture you can see the burning of Old St. Paul's.

THE GREAT PLAGUE

The Bubonic Plague or Black Death first came to Europe and England in 1384 and roughly one third of the population of the country died in two years. The disease reappeared many times in the following 300 years. There was a particularly bad outbreak in London in 1664-5 where it was known as 'The Great Plague.'

THE MONUMENT

This tall column is a monument to the Fire of London and was also designed by Wren. It has a spiral staircase inside and when you get to the top of the 311 steps you will be the same distance above the ground as the base is from the baker's shop in Pudding Lane where the fire is believed to have started.

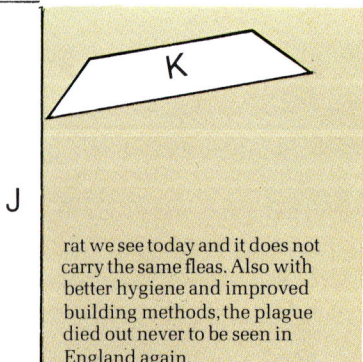

rat we see today and it does not carry the same fleas. Also with better hygiene and improved building methods, the plague died out never to be seen in England again.

The Wellington Monument.

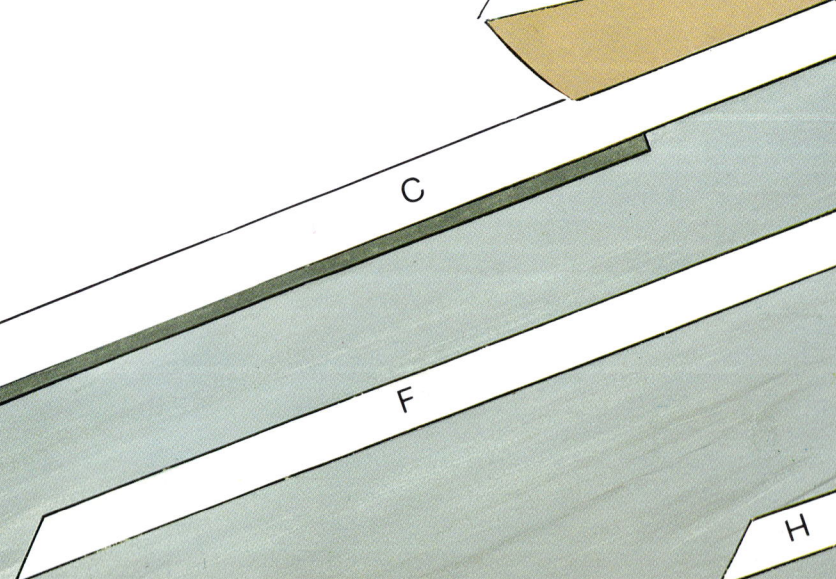

SIR CHRISTOPHER WREN

Sir Christopher Wren was a remarkable man who lived a full and active life. Apart from St. Paul's, he designed 54 other churches in London as well as buildings in Oxford, Cambridge and Greenwich. He started St. Paul's at the age of 36 and was 78 when the last stone was laid. When he died at the age of 91, he was buried in St. Paul's and above the grave can be seen the inscription "Si monumentum requiris, circumspice," which means "If you seek his monument, look around."

THE CITY OF LONDON

The history of London began in 43 AD when the Romans built a bridge across the Thames near the present site of London Bridge. On the north bank the Roman city of Londinium began to grow. By 200 AD the city was surrounded by a strong wall of which traces can still be seen today. The modern City of London roughly lies within the limits of the Roman walls and covers only about one square mile.

After the Great Fire the City developed into a financial and commercial centre which is still one of the greatest in the world. Within the limits of the City are literally hundreds of banks and thousands of offices. The major buildings you can see include the Stock Exchange, the Bank of England, Lloyd's, the Baltic Exchange, The Royal Exchange, the Guildhall and the Mansion House. Both the Stock Exchange and the Guildhall are open to visitors each day.

Within the city is to be found the Central Criminal Court, usually known as the Old Bailey, where important trials are held. You can also see the Head Offices of the National Newspapers in Fleet Street and it is interesting to walk out of the city through the Royal Courts of Justice and into Lincoln's Inn Fields.

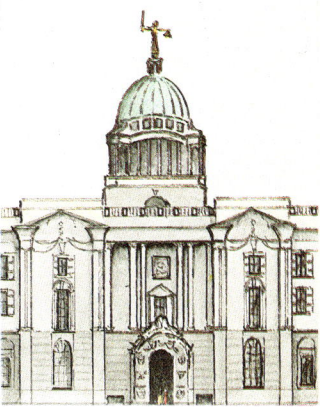

THE LORD MAYOR'S SHOW

Every year a new Lord Mayor of London is elected and in November he drives through the streets of the City in a colourful procession which is known as 'The Lord Mayor's Show.' Later on, he gives a great banquet and it is a well established occasion for important speeches. The home of the Lord Mayor for his year of office is the Mansion House.

ST. PAUL'S CATHEDRAL AND THE LORD MAYOR'S SHOW

SCENE 2 PIECE 4   F   SCORE HILL FOLD   SCORE HILL FOLD   G

SCORE VALLEY FOLD

ST. PAUL'S CATHEDRAL AND THE
LORD MAYOR'S SHOW

L

PLAGUE CARRIERS

SCORE VALLEY FOLD

SCORE HILL FOLD

J

The disease was carried by
particular fleas which lived only
on the black rat, although this
was not known at the time.
Gradually the black rat was
displaced by the common brown

SCENE 2 PIECE 6

SCORE VALLEY FOLD

GLUES BEHIND

WELCOME TO THE LORD MAYOR'S SHOW

SCENE 2 PIECE 7   L   SCORE HILL FOLD   K   SCORE HILL FOLD

CUT HERE

FOLD AND GLUE BACK TO BACK
SCORE HILL FOLD

GLUES BEHIND   E

SCENE 2 PIECE 2   C   SCORE HILL FOLD   SCORE VALLEY FOLD

POP-UP SCENE 3 THE HOUSES OF PARLIAMENT AND WESTMINSTER ABBEY

Looking across Parliament Square this scene shows the Houses of Parliament from Big Ben to the Victoria Tower in all their gothic splendour. To the right, St. Margaret's Westminster is standing in front of Westminster Abbey and in the foreground is the famous statue of Winston Churchill.

For a colour photograph of the completed scene, see inside the back cover.

SCENE 3 POSITION OF THE PIECES

THE HOUSES OF PARLIAMENT There are two Houses of Parliament, the Commons and the Lords, and both meet here in the Palace of Westminster. This view is from Parliament Square and shows the clock tower "Big Ben" at one end and the Victoria Tower at the other. When Parliament is sitting, a flag flies over the Victoria Tower by day and a light shines from Big Ben by night.

Parliament has met on this site since 1547, but the building we see today is relatively new. There was a terrible fire in 1834 and the palace was then rebuilt by Charles Barry. The beautiful river frontage, which is best seen from across the Thames is well worth crossing either the Westminster Bridge or the Lambeth Bridge to see. It is possible to listen to debates in both the Commons and the Lords and sometimes you can visit the magnificent State Rooms and see Westminster Hall, the only part to remain virtually intact since 1399. Westminster Hall is the building which protrudes forward into Parliament Square and was the place where the famous trials of Thomas More, Guy Fawkes and Charles I were held. It is still occasionally used for State functions.

BIG BEN Nowadays people use the name "Big Ben" to mean the clock tower, but strictly it is the name of the large bell on which the hours are struck. The bell weighs 13½ tonnes and was named after Sir Benjamin Hall who was the Commissioner of Works when the tower was erected in 1859. The sound of Big Ben is well known all over the world because it is used for BBC broadcasts.

The power of Parliament steadily increased and came into conflict with the power of the King. In the reign of Charles I this resulted in civil war, which was eventually won by the parliamentarians under Oliver Cromwell. Charles I was tried in the Westminster Hall and then executed in Whitehall on January 30 1649. For eleven years Britain was without a King and was ruled by Cromwell as Lord Protector. On his death the monarchy was restored, but never with the power it had formally had. From the reign of Charles II to the present day, the power of Parliament has remained supreme.

GUY FAWKES AND THE GUNPOWDER PLOT
In 1605 a plot was discovered to blow up the King and the Houses of Parliament with gunpowder hidden in the cellars. Guy Fawkes was arrested in the cellars, tortured and then executed together with some of his associates. This event is celebrated on November 5th yearly with fireworks and bonfires so that "Gunpowder, treason and plot shall never ever be forgot."

This painting of the coronation of William the Conqueror in 1066, clearly shows part of the Abbey still under construction.

WESTMINSTER ABBEY There has been a church on this site since Saxon times. It was rebuilt both before and after the Norman conquest, although most of what we see today was built in the reign of Henry III (1216-1272).

Westminster Abbey is one of the foremost churches in Britain and has been used for the coronation of all kings and queens since William the Conqueror. The coronation throne is a simple wooden throne with the Stone of Scone beneath it. It can be seen at the east end of the Cathedral.

Many royal marriages have also taken place here including that between Queen Elizabeth II and Prince Philip. The Abbey is also a place where many famous people are buried. You will find graves and monuments to kings, queens, princes, statesmen, writers, musicians and of course 'Poet's Corner' which is especially interesting to visit. Just inside the main entrance is the grave of the Unknown Warrior. This simple flat stone, surrounded by poppies, commemorates those who died in the First World War and whose final resting place is unknown.

ST. MARGARET'S OF WESTMINSTER This beautiful church stands in front of the Abbey and was consecrated in 1523. It is now the parish church of the House of Commons. Do check the time shown on the sundials against Big Ben across the square!

EDWARD THE CONFESSOR This saintly man was King of England from 1042 to 1066. He is credited with being the founder of the Palace of Westminster, St. Margaret's Church and Westminster Abbey.

CLEOPATRA'S NEEDLE This granite obelisk, given by Egypt in 1878 now stands on the Embankment not far from Parliament. It is popularly known as "Cleopatra's Needle," although it was already old when she came to the throne.

BOADICEA Just opposite Big Ben, near to Westminster Pier is a statue commemorating Boadicea (Boudicca), a famous queen of the Ancient Britons.

STATUE OF WINSTON CHURCHILL This statue was unveiled in 1973 and symbolises the bulldog spirit and determination with which he steered the country to victory in the second World War.
Churchill is buried at the village church of Bladon in Oxfordshire.

THE HOUSES OF PARLIAMENT AND WESTMINSTER ABBEY

THE HOUSES OF PARLIAMENT AND WESTMINSTER ABBEY

POP-UP SCENE 4 TRAFALGAR SQUARE AND NELSON'S COLUMN

The National Gallery forms the back-drop of this scene of Trafalgar Square looking towards the north, with the fountains and Nelson's column in the foreground. On the day of this scene, a small rally or demonstration is taking attention for a while from all the pigeons which normally make this square their home.

For a colour photograph of the completed scene, see inside the back cover.

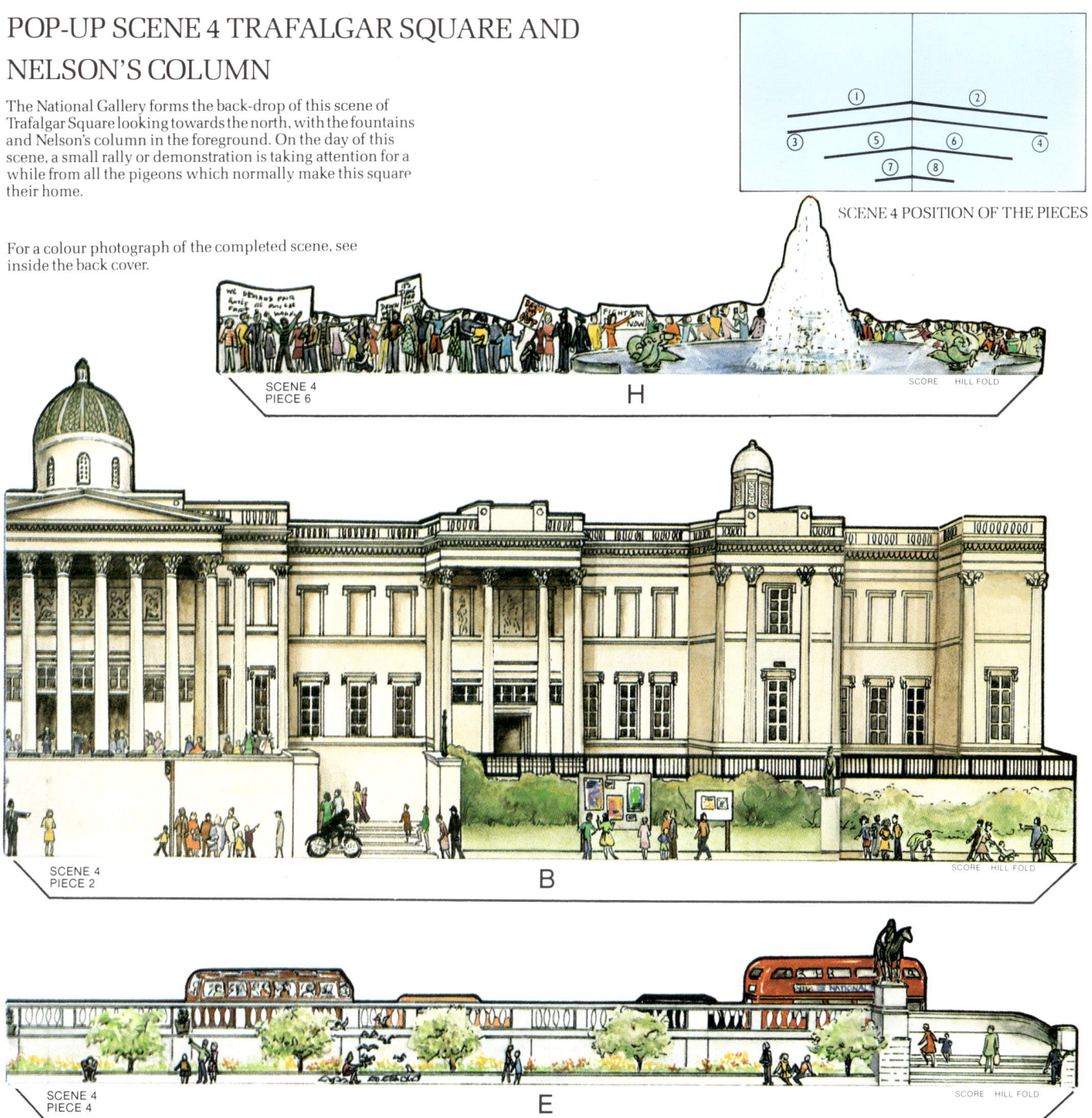

SCENE 4 POSITION OF THE PIECES

SCENE 4 PIECE 6

H

SCORE HILL FOLD

SCENE 4 PIECE 2

B

SCORE HILL FOLD

SCENE 4 PIECE 4

E

SCORE HILL FOLD

HORATIO NELSON
1758-1805

THE BATTLE OF TRAFALGAR
1805

TRAFALGAR SQUARE

Trafalgar Square is a popular place for visitors and this view looking across it to the north shows the National Gallery, the fountains and of course Nelson's Column. The square is named after Nelson's great victory at Trafalgar in 1805. Today it is often used as a meeting place and as a site for rallies and demonstrations. It is also well known for its pigeons and many people come to the Square just to feed them. A special event during December is the erection of a huge decorated Christmas tree, the gift of the people of Norway, and the square then serves as a focus for carol singing and charity collections.

From the square you can look through Admiralty Arch down the Mall towards Buckingham Palace or down Whitehall towards the Houses of Parliament. To the north, behind the National Gallery, lie Leicester Square, Piccadilly Circus and the famous bookshops and music shops of the Charing Cross Road. To the east lie the Strand and Fleet Street with its newspaper offices and to the West St. James's and its royal palace. This is the very heart of London.

HORATIO NELSON

Viscount Horatio Nelson was one of the best loved British commanders and his remarkable victories helped to contain and then defeat the power of Napoleon. He spent most of his short life on active service and was wounded several times, losing an arm and an eye. At the Battle of Trafalgar he was hit again and died a few hours later, but not before he knew he had won a great victory. His body was brought back to England preserved in a cask of brandy and he was buried with full honours in St. Paul's Cathedral.

His flagship, called appropriately enough "The Victory" can still be seen at Portsmouth and there is a vivid tableau at Madame Tussaud's complete with the sound of the actual guns.

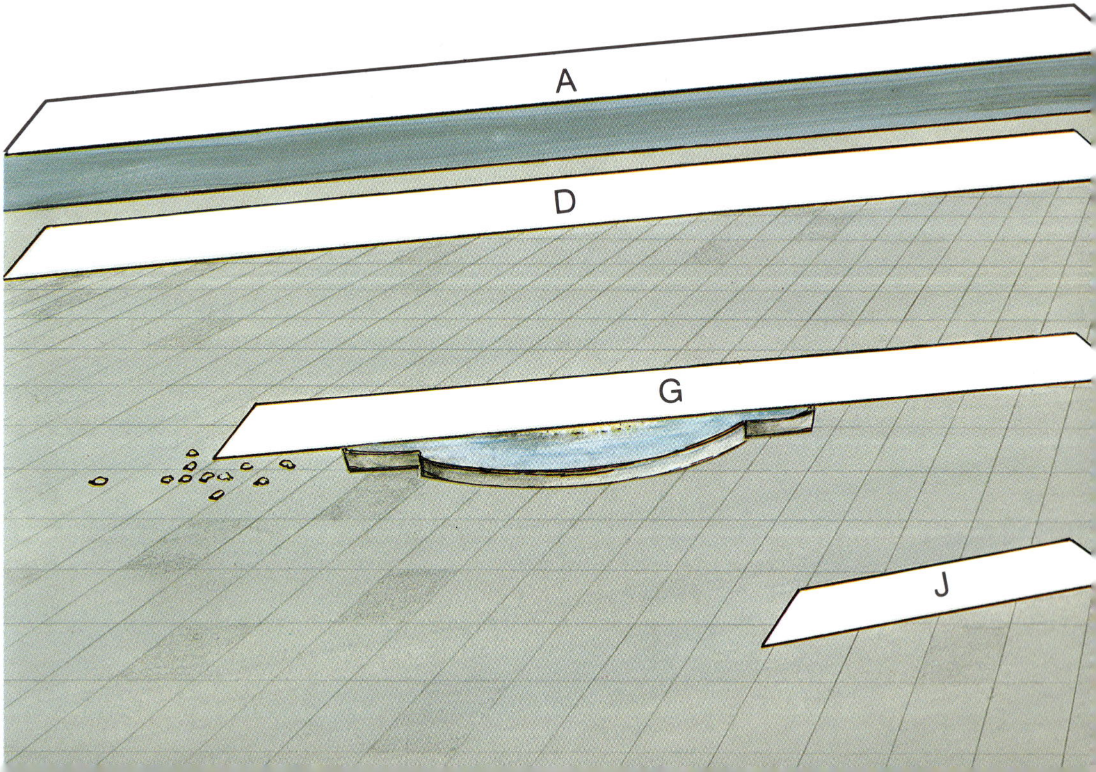

NELSON'S COLUMN

This column which dominates the square is 52 metres high. Around the base are bronze reliefs cast from the metal of captured French guns, and showing scenes from Nelson's victories. The four huge bronze lions which stand on guard at the base were designed by Landseer.

A

D

G

J

THE NATIONAL GALLERY

In this lovely building you can see all the 2000 or more paintings in the National Gallery Collection. Since that would be rather a lot to try to do, they are constantly organising competitions, quizzes, slide shows, guided tours and lectures to help you appreciate what there is to see. Every year the Gallery organises the National Children's Painting Competition.

THE NATIONAL PORTRAIT GALLERY

Here you can see portraits of famous men and women from Tudor times to the present day. Apart from the permanent collection, there are often exhibitions of paintings and photography. The entrance is behind the National Gallery in St. Martin's Place.

THE TATE GALLERY

If you are interested in modern art then this is the best gallery to visit. There is almost always a special exhibition of contemporary art and sculpture taking place.

Three well known pictures which can be seen in the National Gallery

UCCELLO   ST. GEORGE AND THE DRAGON   VAN EYCK   THE ARNOLFINI MARRIAGE
REMBRANDT BELSHAZZAR'S FEAST

B

E

H

K

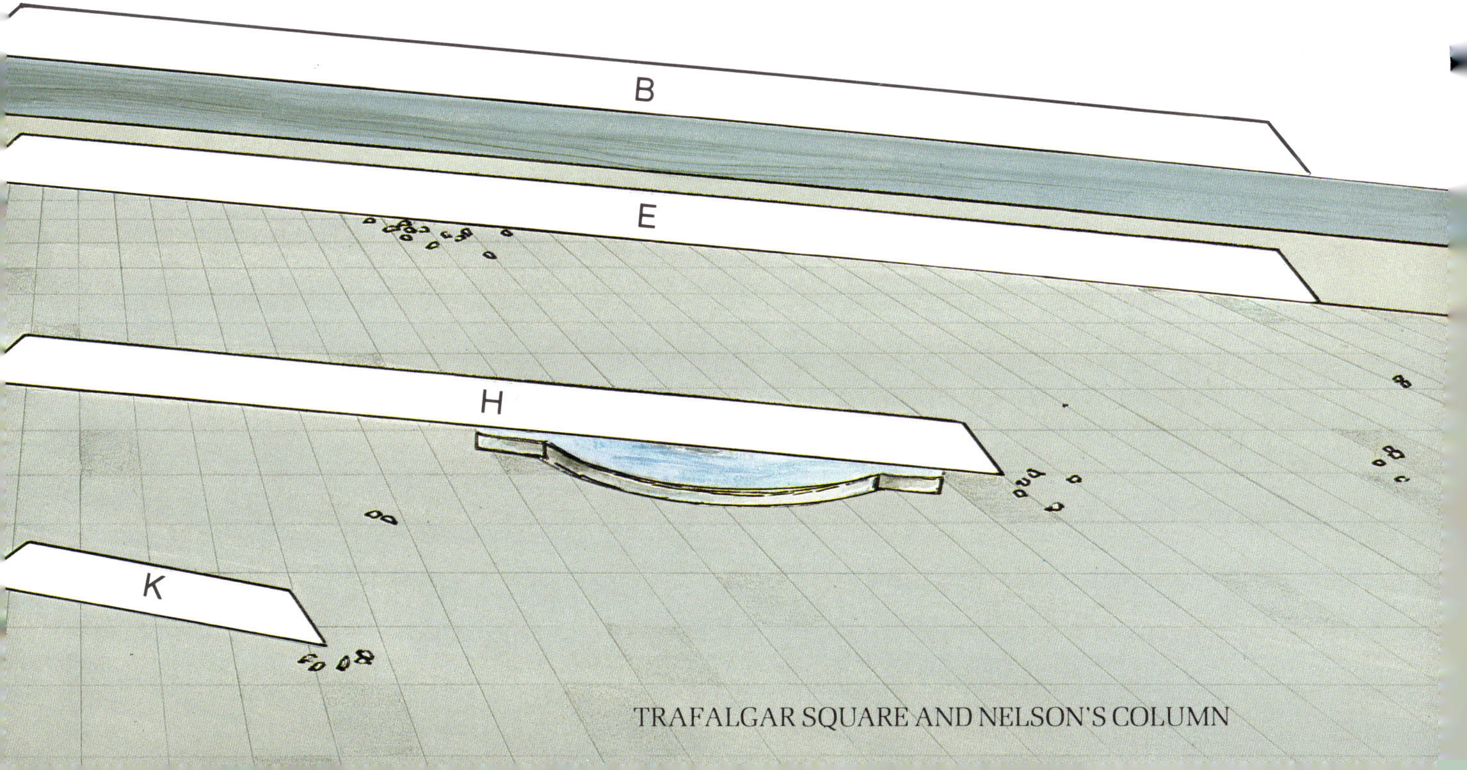

TRAFALGAR SQUARE AND NELSON'S COLUMN

TRAFALGAR SQUARE AND NELSON'S COLUMN

SCENE 4 PIECE 3

D

F

GLUES BEHIND

SCORE HILL FOLD

SCORE VALLEY FOLD

VISIT YOUR NATIONAL GALLERY

SCENE 4 PIECE 1

A

C

GLUES BEHIND

SCORE HILL FOLD

SCORE VALLEY FOLD

SCENE 4 PIECE 5

G

I

GLUES BEHIND

SCORE HILL FOLD

SCORE VALLEY FOLD

SCENE 4 PIECE 8

K

SCORE HILL FOLD

SCENE 4 PIECE 7

J

L

GLUES BEHIND

SCORE HILL FOLD

POP-UP SCENE 5 BUCKINGHAM PALACE AND THE VICTORIA MONUMENT

The royal standard flies above Buckingham Palace as the royal coach passes by. In the foreground of this scene stands the Victoria monument, a favourite spot for tourists and visitors on royal occasions. And a mini pop-up shows another attraction for visitors, one of the Foot Guards on sentry duty in his colourful uniform and bearskin hat.

SCENE 5 POSITION OF THE PIECES

For a colour photograph of the completed scene, see inside the back cover.

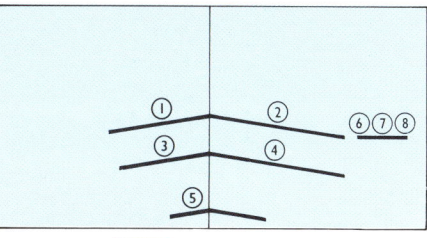

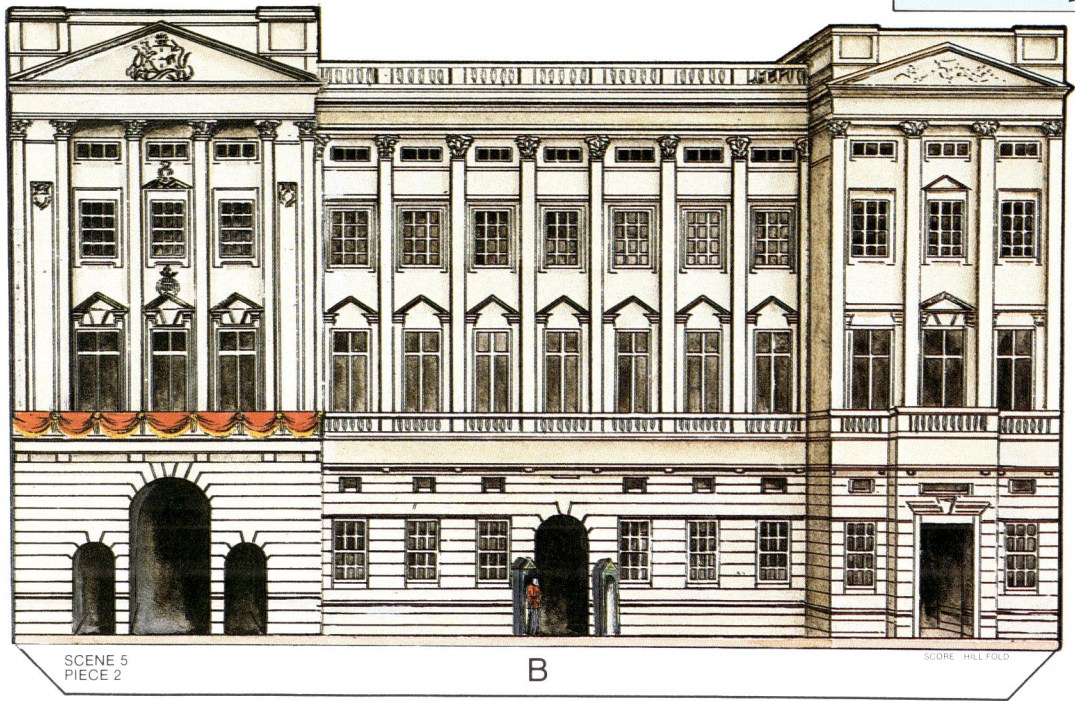

SCENE 5
PIECE 2

B

SCORE HILL FOLD

GLUES
BEHIND

SCENE 5
THE ROYAL STANDARD FLIES
ABOVE THE CENTRE OF THE
PALACE

SCENE 5
PIECE 4

E

SCORE HILL FOLD

BUCKINGHAM PALACE

The Palace, or 'Buck House' as it is sometimes affectionately known, is the official residence of the Royal Family in London. Tradition decrees that the royal standard flies over the palace only when the King or Queen is in residence. On special occasions, the royal family appear on the balcony to wave to the crowds or to take the salute at an R.A.F. flypast. Surrounding the palace are extensive gardens and a lake with the famous pink flamingoes. It is in these gardens that the Royal Garden parties are held for people being given special honours.

Buckingham Palace was not always a royal residence, nor did it always look as it does today. This drawing shows how it looked about 300 years ago. It became a royal palace when it was bought in 1761 by George III from the Duke of Buckingham.

The Royal family also have other palaces where they spend part of the time and where they can escape from the more formal atmosphere of Buckingham Palace. Sandringham in Norfolk and Balmoral in Scotland are particular favourites.

WINDSOR CASTLE lies to the west of London overlooking the river Thames, and parts of it are open when members of the royal family are not in residence. It is possible to see the magnificent state apartments, St. George's Chapel, and the Round Tower and Curfew Tower.

HAMPTON COURT is no longer used by the royal family but is well worth a visit. It was built by Cardinal Wolsey and was given by him to Henry VIII. One famous attraction here is the maze, where it is only too easy to get lost. You can also see the court where Henry VIII played an early form of tennis.

THE QUEEN'S GALLERY

An old Chapel in the south wing of the Palace has been converted into a Gallery where many of the wonderful pictures and treasures of the royal collection are on show. It is the only part of the Palace which is ever open to the public.

THE ROYAL MEWS

On certain afternoons it is possible to visit the Royal Mews and to see the magnificent horses and carriages used in state processions.

BRITISH SOVEREIGNS

William the Conqueror
1066-1087

Richard the Lionheart
1189-1199

Richard III
1483-1485

The British Monarchy has a very long history indeed, going back to Egbert, the first King of the English in 827.

These six portraits show some well known sovereigns who made their mark on the history of their country for good or evil.

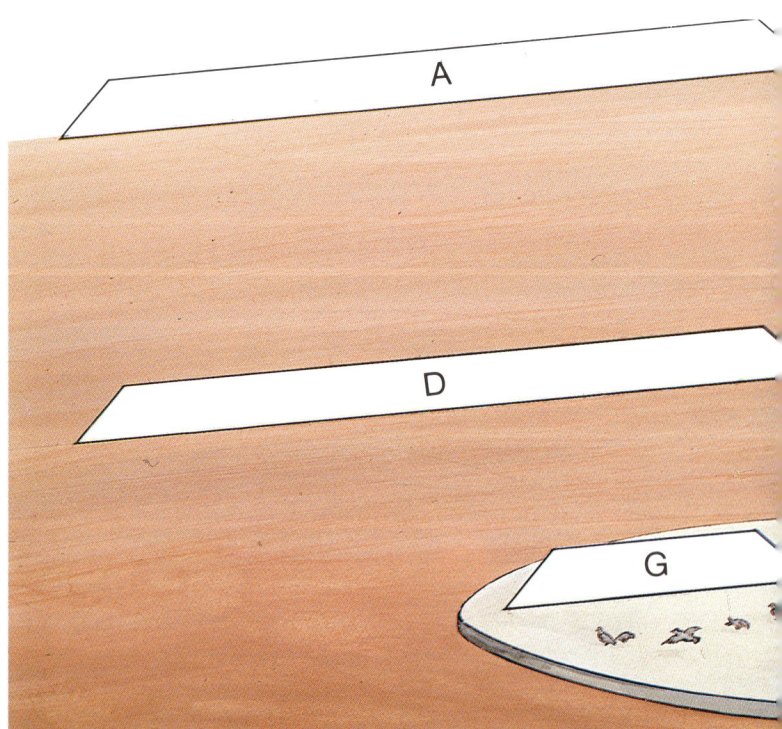

Elizabeth I
1588-1603

Charles I
1625-1649

THE HOUSEHOLD BRIGADE

On ceremonial occasions, the personal bodyguard of the sovereign is provided by the Household Brigade. This colourful Brigade consists of two regiments of cavalry and five regiments of Foot guards. The cavalry are the Life Guards, who wear scarlet jackets and white plumes and the Royal Horse Guards who wear blue jackets and red plumes are known as "The Blues."

Trooping the colour takes place in June each year and is a very colourful event.

The ceremonial changing of the guard at Buckingham Palace takes place daily at Buckingham Palace, and in Whitehall at the Horse Guards.

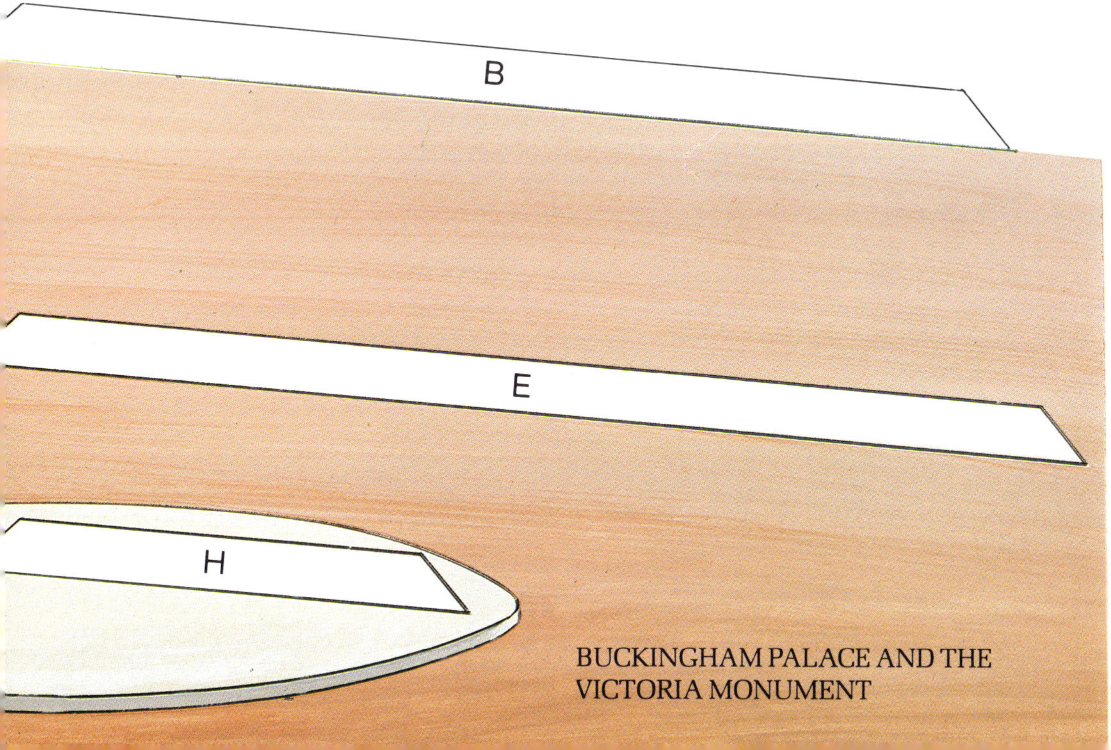

B

GUARDS TABLEAU   L

E

H

THE GUARDS

All the Foot Guards wear the same scarlet jackets and busbies, but each regiment has a different arrangement of buttons. They are called the Grenadier, Coldstream, Scots, Irish and Welsh Guards. In London they are an important part of pageantry, but for each individual guardsman it is only a part of his duties. They are crack regiments of the British Army, and training in the use of modern weapons is as important as drill with sword and rifle.

BUCKINGHAM PALACE AND THE VICTORIA MONUMENT

BUCKINGHAM PALACE AND THE
VICTORIA MONUMENT

SCORE
VALLEY FOLD

C

GLUES
BEHIND

SCENE 5
PIECE 1

A

G

SCENE 5
PIECE 5

H

J

GLUES
BEHIND

K

SCENE 5
PIECE 8

GOD BLESS OUR
GRACIOUS QUEEN

F

GLUES
BEHIND

SCENE 5
PIECE 3

D

SCENE 5
PIECE 7

L

I

POP-UP SCENE 6 CENTRAL LONDON, A VISITOR'S GUIDE

For a colour photograph of the completed scene, see inside the back cover.

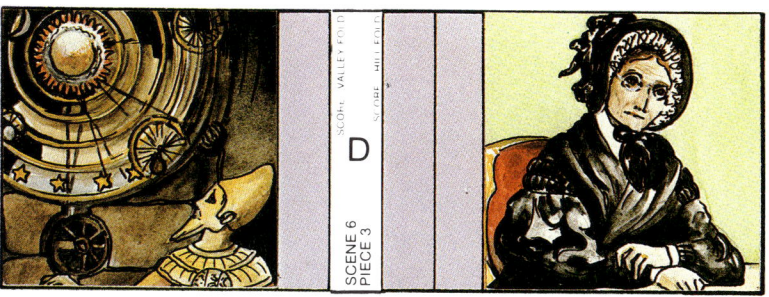

SCORE VALLEY FOLD
SCORE HILL FOLD
D
SCENE 6 PIECE 3

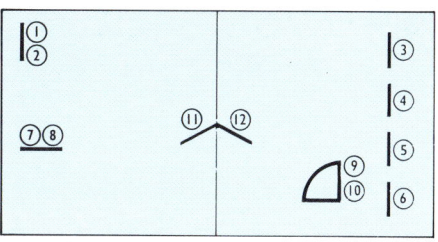

SCENE 6 POSITION OF THE PIECES

Grouped around a visitor's map of central London, this scene shows a wealth of ideas and suggestions of interesting places to visit or things to do. The statue of Eros in Piccadilly Circus dominates the scene, but there are mini pop-ups of the Zoo, London Transport and the Museum of London, not forgetting the four flip-flop flaps!

BRASS RUBBING
Many people find this an interesting activity and you can try it at St. James's Church Hall in Piccadilly or in the cloisters of Westminster Abbey. All materials are supplied.

SCORE VALLEY FOLD
SCORE HILL FOLD
E
SCENE 6 PIECE 4

MARIONETTE THEATRE
The Little Angel Marionette Theatre is one of the very few theatres solely devoted to puppetry in all its forms. The theatre seats 100 and there are shows every weekend and daily during school holidays.

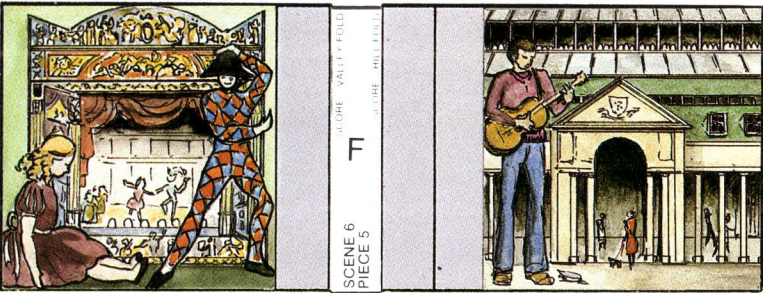

SCORE VALLEY FOLD
SCORE HILL FOLD
F
SCENE 6 PIECE 5

WATER BUSES
A lovely way to get to the Zoo or just to see a little known part of London.
You can also follow the same route along the Regent's Park or Grand Union Canals on foot.

SCORE VALLEY FOLD
SCORE HILL FOLD
G
SCENE 6 PIECE 6

THE LONDON DUNGEON
Gruesome horrors of the middle ages from tortures and ordeals to dreadful diseases are all displayed in dank and dismal alcoves. A place you will either love or hate.

SCENE 6 PIECE 12 M
SCORE HILL FOLD

SCENE 6 PIECE 11 L
SCORE HILL FOLD

SCORE VALLEY FOLD
N
GLUES BEHIND

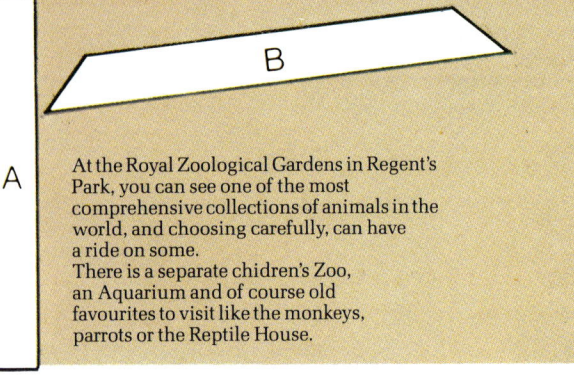

A

B

At the Royal Zoological Gardens in Regent's Park, you can see one of the most comprehensive collections of animals in the world, and choosing carefully, can have a ride on some.
There is a separate chidren's Zoo, an Aquarium and of course old favourites to visit like the monkeys, parrots or the Reptile House.

PICCADILLY CIRCUS AND EROS
It is said that if you wait at Piccadilly Circus long enough, you will meet everyone you know. It is a popular meeting place, well known for its bright lights, cinemas, theatres, shops and restaurants.
The statue of Eros is a monument to Lord Shaftesbury, the reformer who did so much to improve the lives of men, women and children. Apparently the sculptor thought of the statue as Charity, flying swift as an arrow to help people.

LONDON TRANSPORT TABLEAU   J

THE UNDERGROUND
No fewer than nine separate underground or 'tube' lines pass under central London and this means that nowhere is far from a station. The different lines are connected by escalators and stairways so there is no difficulty in changing from one line to another and getting to your destination. For most people making their first visit to London, the underground is often just as exciting as the famous sights on the ground above.

LONDON BUSES
Bright red double decker buses are a well known feature of the London scene. And being above ground you can see some famous buildings as you travel to others!

L

ST. KATHARINE DOCKS
Just to the east of the Tower is a series of yacht harbours and linked walkways. It is a fascinating place to explore, with boats of every kind to see. There is also an historic ship collection where each vessel can be visited and you can return to the river bank and Tower Bridge via the old lock gates.

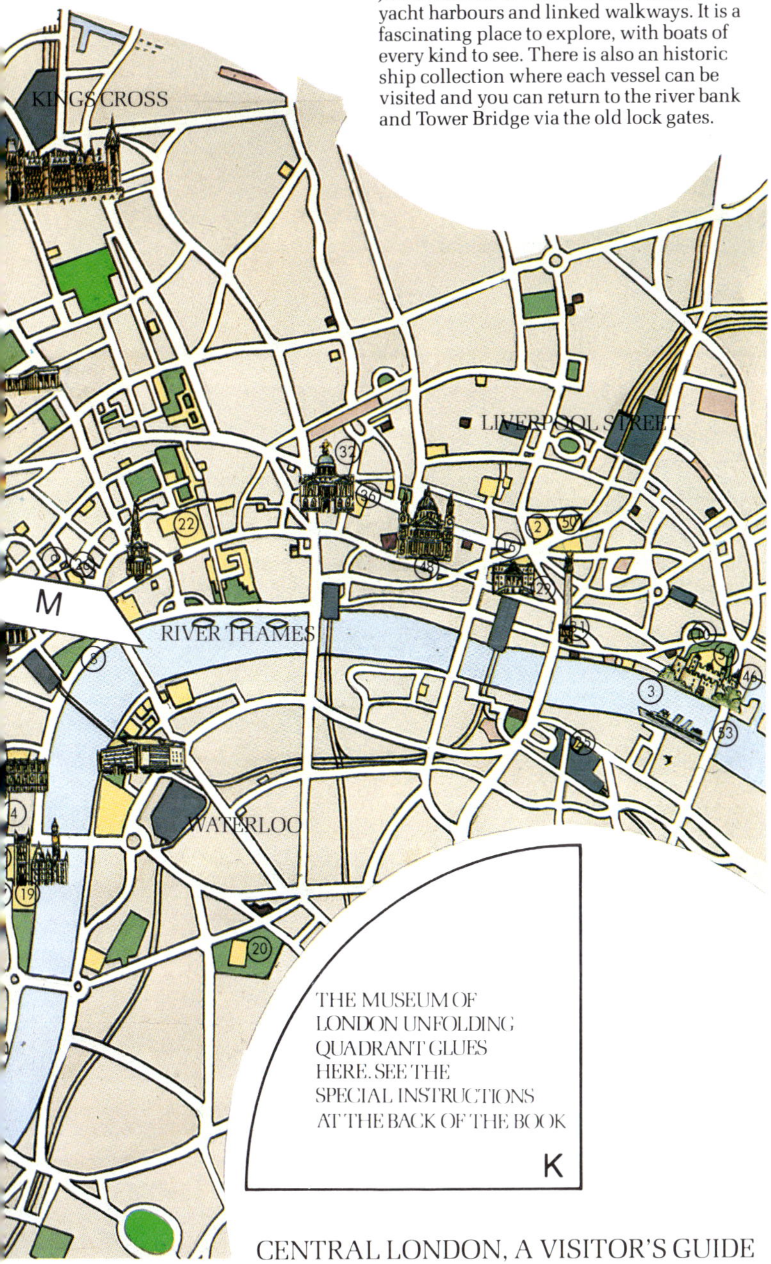

THE MUSEUM OF LONDON UNFOLDING QUADRANT GLUES HERE.. SEE THE SPECIAL INSTRUCTIONS AT THE BACK OF THE BOOK

K

CENTRAL LONDON, A VISITOR'S GUIDE

PLACES AND PLEASURE...
These four flip-flop flaps show eight more places which attract many, many visitors each year.

MADAME TUSSAUD'S
Kings, queens, sportsmen, heroes, villains and murderers, are all presented as life size wax works in scenes and tableaux. Don't miss the Chamber of Horrors or the battle of Trafalgar!

D

THE PLANETARIUM
The sky at night, presented during the day! A special projector creates images of the planets, moon and stars on the roof of the dome and shows how they change with the unfolding year. Visit the Astronomer's Gallery.

E

COVENT GARDEN
The old fruit and vegetable market buildings have been converted into a delightful shopping precinct and market. There are usually musicians, singers, dancers or buskers somewhere in the vicinity.

F

POLLOCKS TOY MUSEUM
There is a museum of historical toys, dolls and theatres of all kinds in Scala Street and a shop in the Covent Garden precinct.

G

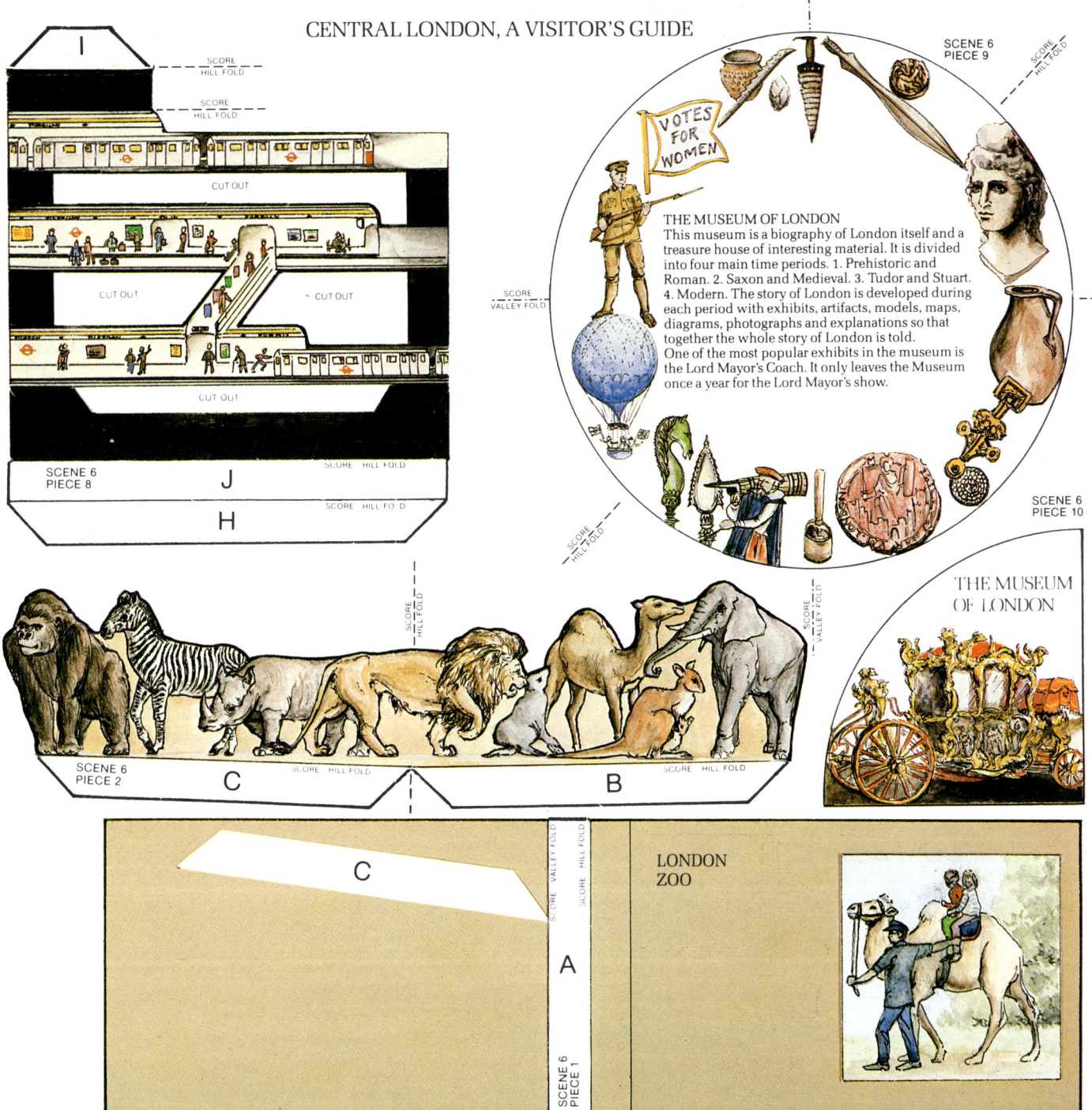

SCORE HILL FOLD

SCORE HILL FOLD

I

CUT OUT

CUT OUT

CUT OUT

CUT OUT

CUT OUT

SCENE 6
PIECE 8

J

SCORE HILL FOLD

SCORE HILL FO D

H

VOTES FOR WOMEN

SCORE VALLEY FOLD

THE MUSEUM OF LONDON

This museum is a biography of London itself and a treasure house of interesting material. It is divided into four main time periods. 1. Prehistoric and Roman. 2. Saxon and Medieval. 3. Tudor and Stuart. 4. Modern. The story of London is developed during each period with exhibits, artifacts, models, maps, diagrams, photographs and explanations so that together the whole story of London is told.

One of the most popular exhibits in the museum is the Lord Mayor's Coach. It only leaves the Museum once a year for the Lord Mayor's show.

SCENE 6
PIECE 9

SCORE HILL FOLD

SCORE HILL FOLD

SCENE 6
PIECE 10

THE MUSEUM OF LONDON

SCENE 6
PIECE 2

C

SCORE HILL FOLD

SCORE HILL FOLD

B

SCORE HILL FOLD

SCORE VALLEY FOLD

C

SCORE VALLEY FOLD

SCORE HILL FOLD

A

SCENE 6
PIECE 1

LONDON ZOO

MINI-COVERS FOR MINI POP-UPS

These five covers are for additional mini pop-ups on certain scenes. First cut the whole page from the book. Then cut out the individual pieces looking at the other side.

Its story began with William the Conqueror in 1066. Soon after his victory at Hastings, he came to London to make it his capital and began building the Tower even before his coronation. At first it consisted of the White Tower only, a central keep surrounded by a palisade of wood and earth and a moat, but in the following centuries more and more towers and walls were added.

In its time, the Tower has served as a palace, the mint, a zoo, a prison and a place of murder and execution. The Crown Jewels were brought here from Westminster Abbey in 1303 and have been here ever since. Nowadays it is a museum, with one of the best collections of Armour anywhere, and a place for visitors to imagine events from the past which took place here. Events like the murder of the Princes in the Tower, the torturing of Guy Fawkes, the imprisonment of Sir Walter Raleigh for thirteen years, and of course the execution of Anne Boleyn.

THE TRAITOR'S GATE

In the past the river ran close to the walls of the Tower and prisoners were brought directly by boat to this gate. Today the embankment has been built up and you can approach it on foot and look from this entrance into the Tower.

LONDON TRANSPORT MUSEUM

Situated in Covent Garden this museum offers a complete history of public transport in the London area. Many ancient vehicles have been preserved and others rescued from the scrapheap and carefully restored. There are horse buses, horse trams, early motor and electric vehicles and some of the first underground carriages. There are many working models and you can 'drive' a bus or a tube train, change the signals or alter the points. There are old photographs and maps and examples of many kinds of machine, tickets, handbills and posters.

GREENWICH

MINI-COVERS FOR MINI POP-UPS

After removing the whole page from the book, cut out the five individual pieces looking at this side.

SCENE 5
PIECE 1
G

H

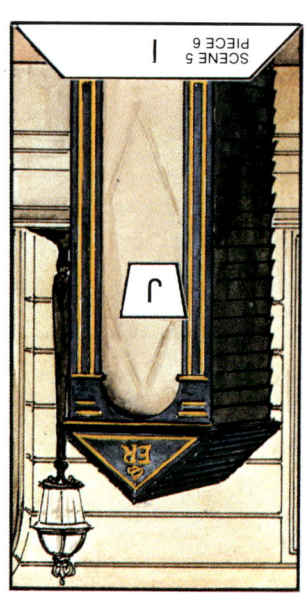

SCENE 5
PIECE 6
I

J

SCENE 1
PIECE 9
K

L

SCENE 6
PIECE 7
H

I

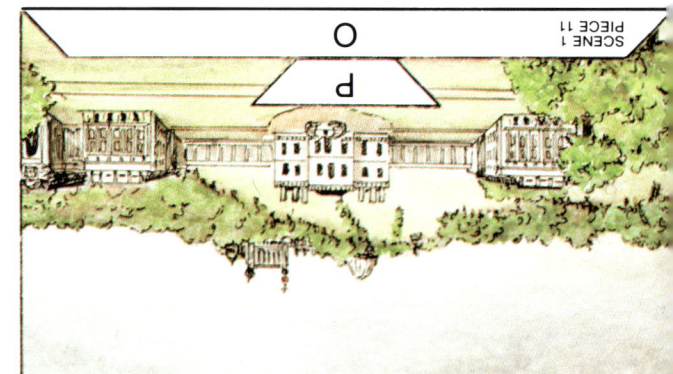

SCENE 1
PIECE 11
O

P

HOW TO MAKE THE MINI POP-UPS

Apart from the six main scenes, there are some extra mini pop-ups each of which adds its contribution to the fascinating story of London. There are three different types, which are called (a) The tableaux, (b) The matching frames, (c) The unfolding quadrant.
Follow the instructions on this page to make them.

TO MAKE THE TABLEAUX

Scene 1 Anne Boleyn	Pieces 5, 6, 7
Scene 1 Beefeaters	Pieces 8, 9 10
Scene 1 Greenwich	Pieces 11, 12, 13
Scene 5 The Guards	Pieces 6, 7, 8
Scene 6 London Transport	Pieces 7, 8

1. Cut out the pieces which make each tableau.
2. Score and fold as indicated. All are hill folds. Crease firmly.
3. Glue the flaps together in alphabetical order.

These sketches show the side views of the tableaux mini pop-ups when upright and when half-closed. Note how the small support is parallel to the base. It will fold completely flat.

4. When each tableau is complete it can be glued into position on the base.

TO MAKE THE MATCHING FRAMES

Scene 2 The Plague	Pieces 6, 7
Scene 6 London Zoo	Pieces 1, 2
Scene 6 Flip-flop flaps	Pieces 3, 4, 5, 6

1. Cut out the rectangles which form the lids of each mini pop-up or the flip flop flaps.
2. Score along the centre fold line, fold in half and check that the two halves match.

3. Smoothly spread glue inside the fold. Press down and wait till dry.
4. Score along the line marked 'valley fold' and crease gently.
5. Glue into position on the base and then complete the mini pop-ups.

TO MAKE THE UNFOLDING QUADRANT

Scene 6 Museum of London Pieces 9, 10

1. Cut out both pieces keeping well away from the outline.
2. Score along the three diagonals which are marked and crease firmly into hill and valley folds.
3. Cut out precisely.

4. Fold into the quadrant or quarter circle shape as shown in the sketch and glue into position on the base in Scene 6. Check that the print is up the right way when it is opened.
5. Glue the Lord Mayor's Coach on top to complete the mini pop-up.

AND FINALLY

When all these mini pop-ups are complete and you have finished with these instructions, spread glue on the blue tone around the page and glue it to the blank page opposite. Scene 6 then can be completed by glueing Eros into position.

HAVE YOU SEEN?

Here is an alphabetical check list of places in London which are mentioned in this book
or which you could see on a visit.
Of course not everyone is interested in everything or would ever have the time to see them all.
You might however like to tick off those things you have seen, or to use this list to plan a future visit.

- [ ] 1. Albert Hall and Memorial
- [ ] 2. Bank of England
- [ ] 3. Belfast H.M.S.
- [ ] 4. Big Ben
- [ ] 5. British Museum
- [ ] 6. Buckingham Palace
- [ ] 7. Changing the Guard
- [ ] 8. Cleopatra's Needle
- [ ] 9. Covent Garden Precinct
- [ ] 10. Crown Jewels
- [ ] 11. Cutty Sark
- [ ] 12. Downing Street
- [ ] 13. Foot Guards
- [ ] 14. Geffrye Museum
- [ ] 15. Geological Museum
- [ ] 16. Guildhall
- [ ] 17. Hampton Court Palace
- [ ] 18. Horse Guards
- [ ] 19. Houses of Parliament
- [ ] 20. Imperial War Museum
- [ ] 21. Kew Gardens
- [ ] 22. Law Courts
- [ ] 23. Little Angel Theatre
- [ ] 24. London Brass Rubbing
- [ ] 25. London Dungeon
- [ ] 26. London Transport Museum
- [ ] 27. London Zoo
- [ ] 28. Madame Tussaud's
- [ ] 29. Mansion House
- [ ] 30. Marble Arch
- [ ] 31. Monument
- [ ] 32. Museum of London
- [ ] 33. National Gallery
- [ ] 34. Natural History Museum
- [ ] 35. National Maritime Museum
- [ ] 36. Old Bailey
- [ ] 37. Old Royal Observatory
- [ ] 38. Piccadilly Circus
- [ ] 39. Planetarium
- [ ] 40. Pollocks Toy Museum
- [ ] 41. Post Office Tower
- [ ] 42. Queen's Gallery
- [ ] 43. Regent's Canal
- [ ] 44. Royal Airforce Museum
- [ ] 45. Royal Mews
- [ ] 46. St. Katharine's Dock
- [ ] 47. St. Margaret's—Westminster
- [ ] 48. St. Paul's Cathedral
- [ ] 49. Science Museum
- [ ] 50. Stock Exchange
- [ ] 51. Speakers Corner
- [ ] 52. Tate Gallery
- [ ] 53. Tower Bridge
- [ ] 54. Tower of London
- [ ] 55. Trafalgar Square
- [ ] 56. Victoria and Albert Museum
- [ ] 57. Westminster Abbey
- [ ] 58. Westminster Cathedral
- [ ] 59. Windsor Castle
- [ ] 60. Winston Churchill Statue